Pieces of a Broken Soul

Jennifer Dante

Pieces of a Broken Soul

Cover Art by Brianna Hughes

Edited by Tevya O'Quain

Format by Ashley Nemer

ISBN-13:9780615906409

ISBN-10:0615906400

A product of the
Seraphim Treasure

Published November, 2013

DEDICATION

This is dedicated to those who believed in me and my writing.

Voices

Doubt
Jealous
Insecurity
Rage
Distrust
Negativity

These are the voices that haunt us
Toy with us
They lie in wait
For the perfect time
To creep up
To take us down
Piece by piece
Until we are nothing
But a shell
Of our formal selves

Moment

There is something in that moment
Our moment, our connection
Your scent filling my senses
Your taste on my lips
Your sounds traveling to my ears
It all draws me deeper to you

The curves of your breast
The angles of your hips
The sweet flesh of folds between your legs
Is my undoing

Your desire, your need to my own overwhelms us both

Jennifer Dante

Absent

Throat raw
Voice hoarse
Eyes swollen
Body shaken

Everything had fallen away
Slipping like pieces of thread
Thru my fingers

Everything that was known
That gave comfort
Is gone.

Lost

What are you supposed to do when ...

...you've lost your way?
...everything seems to be slipping away?
...you can't find a silver lining in the clouds?
...you're afraid nothing might not work out?
...you can't stay positive anymore?

What does one do with these unanswered questions?

Phoenix

Like a phoenix
Who takes its last breath of air
Turns to a pile of ash
Another life ended

A flame bursts out
A new life starting
The phoenix rises again
Starting its life over

She too will rise again
Looking to the light
Shedding everything weighing her down
Clearing away the spider webs

She hopes to get it right
And like the phoenix
She will keep on
Making a new start over and over
Until everything is right

Wanted

Is it that you wanted...longed for...
Pain of a flog or sting of her bite
Burn of the rope or smack of the paddle
Is it the heat you want, or shivers down your back?
Her growl or Her whispers…
To be the good girl and get worshiped
or a bad girl and be punished
What is it that you want?

Jennifer Dante

Reflection

Is it true, the beauty in the eye of the beholder?
What if the beholder is oneself?
Do the rules still apply, or just to someone looking at them?

Stripped away and free of the makeup
The label you wear on your body
The hair pulled back in the simple ponytail

What do you see when looking down yourself
Or at your reflection in the mirror?

Do you see a flat stomach?
Do you see a little extra around the hips?
Do you have "tiger stripes" from the birth of your children?

What if you see yourself differently from what people say?
What do you say to them?
Thank you or no I do not agree?

Do you tear up seeing your reflection?
Wanting to hide yourself from everyone?
Due to a false body image
Thinking you aren't worth it?

When I look at my reflection
I see scars, both on my skin and invisible ones
I see an imperfect body
Wishing I could scrub away the imperfections

When I look at my reflection
I see my grandmother's nose
Plain, thick brown hair, the tips kissing my shoulders
Eyes color of mud, that at times are lifeless

When I look at my reflection
I see my own tiger stripes that gave my son life
Hips that brought him forth to the world

Pieces of a Broken Soul

Thick thighs on short muscle legs

Is this reflection true?
It's hard to say
Maybe you can tell me if I'm wrong?

Pleasure

"Show Me.." She said, and I tried to hide the blush on my cheek, hiding my face..

"Higher.." She said, and I pressed my hardening nipples into cool surface..

"Wider.." and I lost the battle to hide the arousal between my legs as I spread them part

"That's it.. you're wet. Moist... are ready for me? "

"Show Me .. My pet.. that's it.." She said, as I raised my ass higher into the air, on display for her

"It's beautiful.." she said, her voice full of pride.. "And all Mine.."

Jennifer Dante

Safe

She puts up walls around her
To protect her from various things

She shelters herself from storms,
The demons that like to creep up
Who like to play with her emotions and her mind

People have tried to break down her walls
Layer by layer
To get to know the person behind it

When she feels them breaking down
She quickly puts them back up again
The walls make her feel safe, protected

People say she is strong,
That she does not need them

She only exposes her true self to a few
Ones that have stood by her, flaws and all

Those are the people that are allowed inside her walls

Façade

Screaming against the invisible four walls around me
Hot streams of tears running down my cheeks
Fists swing out trying to knock it down
Only to hit and miss

Coursing through my body
A feeling of being trapped
Unable to get out

Loneliness flooding my heart
Doubt joining in
My heart breaking in uneven pieces

Anger joins in the miss that is me
My blood boiling
Thinking that you did this to me.

Standing in the middle of the room
I let out a cry, ear shattering scream
The invisible breaking down
Invisible pieces flying around me

Quiet Ones

You think we don't know

It's the quiet ones like me
One has to look out for

You think we don't find out

Always keeping our ears open
Hearing the careless whispers you tell others

You think we don't pay attention

Jennifer Dante

We see things one does not realize
Paying attention to things going around

You think we don't know what's going on

One day, it will all come tumbling down around you
Lies will eat you up, karma will come after you

We the quiet ones will see it
And simply laugh

Fresh Start

The time has come
To strip away the old, dead layers of one's self
Wash away all the mistakes
Negativity and the wrongs
Push the hurt of the past behind you
It's in the past, let it stay there

Put away the demons
The jealousy
The doubt
The hate
They won't come along in the new year

Give thanks for the new beginning
Your friendships
Your loved ones
All the good and positive things you have

Tomorrow is a brand new start
Wake up tomorrow, ready to start again
And good things will come your way

Perfect

I don't claim to be perfect
I never will be
I don't always say the right things
I have many times put my foot in my mouth
I make mistakes like any other person
I try and limit the mistakes as best as I can
I am at fault, I will admit it
When that's the case, I do whatever it takes to make things right
I try to go out of my way for anyone in need
Friend or otherwise
I wear my heart on my sleeve
At times I can be emotional, pouring out everything to my heart's
content.
I love everything in my life with my being
I can get jealous
I can get things confused
Get my facts mixed up
I can say things without thinking about them first
I am only human, I can't be perfect
I can only be me
Take me as I am or don't take me at all

In the Darkness
Standing in a darken room
I look over at the bed
At the face I met seven years ago

My heart aches for both us
I hate that I can't give you
Life I had growing up

I hate that I can't give you everything
your small heart wants

In the darkness I cry
wanting to give you a better life

I feel like I let you down
I let myself down as well

Being a single mother to my child
It wasn't what I wanted nor planned

I look at all the families around me
My heart aches, knowing I had that
And it all slipped away

I hate crying in front of you
Then to have you ask "Why you crying mommy?"

It pained me to think it was your fault
It was never you fault for what happened

I pray, hope and dream of one day
Giving you a better life soon

Dream

I may never have a published novel
I may never have a published story
I may never be a have a single thing written for the whole world to
see under my name

Should I care?
Maybe?
Maybe not?

I know I'm not one of the best writers out there
I know my stories may not be as creative as others
I know I am the only person who is supportive of my doing

But the few words that tumble out of my mouth
mean something to me
They are words that are behind a feeling, a reason for writing them.

They are a small way of expressing something that I have to let out. Yes the words I speak might have a hidden meaning, but it is to each person who reads them to find their own meaning behind it.

In the end I could be standing on a bunch of meaningless words for a few people that read them
However if that is meant to be, then so be it.
I'll keep the dream , will only be just a dream

Confused

You say one thing to me
Then mean another

I am not a toy with a string
To pull at a moment's notice
Thinking I would come running to you

A broken promise here and there
Added with your lies
I will not believe you again

I was not born yesterday
I am much smarter than you think

Your chances are now limited
Keep playing your games
And see what happens

Belonging

I long to be someone's one
I long to hear the word MINE

I willing give myself over
My mind, body, and trust

Jennifer Dante

I long to feel a command in my ear
I long to a be tested

My body to experience both pleasure and pain
To feel the sting on my sensitive, tender parts of my flesh

Stand Before Me

Don't stand before me
Acting like you are better
Than me as person and a parent

Don't stand before me
Spilling your lies
When I've caught you in them over and over

Don't stand before me
Claiming you are struggling like I am
You know what you left me with

Don't stand before me
Stating you want to change
Then don't do anything about it

Don't stand before me
I don't want to see you
Anymore

Do stand before me
I want you to feel the pain
You left me with

Do stand before me
I want you to feel my rage
I have for you

Turn your back on me

Pieces of a Broken Soul

It's all I see since you left me

I no longer want to deal with you!

Just a girl

She is just a girl
Nothing special about her
Brown eyes and hair
Average looking

She encloses walls around her
Afraid of being hurt
For hurt is all she knows from people

She wears her emotions on her sleeve
She is loyal and loves her few friends
With her whole heart
Willing to do anything for anyone in need

She has been through a lot in her short life
Cheating, lying, betrayal
She has her demons just like everyone else
Sometimes she has a hard time battling them back

She is afraid
She is jealous
She is depressed
She is weak

She wishes to be the girl that everyone knows
She wishes to be the girl that is popular
She wishes to be the girl that has lots of friends
She wishes to be the girl who is not now

Her few friends might say something different
However it is hard for her to believe those words

Jennifer Dante

Many times she feels alone
Afraid to speak out and ask for help
She does not like being weak

But that is all she feels at the moment
Weak and alone

Untitled

Love and sand are alike
Give it care and attention,
And it will stay with you

If you are foolish with it
All it takes strong gust of wind
And it you lose it

Everything happens for a reason

The moment one's life came into existence
Family one was raised in

Childhood best friend was the quiet person over the loud one
Attended the private over the public one
First crush one this one over that one
Went to all the high school dances but one of them

The friendships that were made and stayed
The friendships that came and left
The friendship you longed to have again
The friendship you shouldn't have but did anyway
Along with all the fights
Saying something when you shouldn't

Everything happens for a reason....

Pieces of a Broken Soul

One person that was important to one, they left when you needed
them the most
One person you let get away
One person you stayed with to be happy
One person that you can't live without
One person that you hate but still stay friends with them
One person that you love secretly but never tell them

Everything happens for a reason....

Thinking about someone when you shouldn't be
Falling in love with someone when you shouldn't be
Marring the wrong person over the right one
Loving the right person but also loving the wrong
Wishing you could have feelings for someone else than one you have
them for

Everything happens for a reason

There is a reason for me writing this....

On the edge

Standing on the ledge
One step forward
I fall into darkness
One step back
I'm not sure if I want to be there either
Feelings of numbness, pain
surround me

I put on a fake smile and laugh
Hiding my true feelings
Afraid if one heard the truth
Another crack would form
So I kept my distance at arms left
I have someone but not really

Jennifer Dante

When I feel myself breaking apart
I wish I had someone to hold me
Tell me it will be ok
Tell me that I'm safe
Tell me they love me
Even when I don't love myself

Afraid of being alone
Showing that vulnerable part of me
Will that someone leave me
Once they realize how broken I really am
That would be my undoing

Never Know

You'll never know
How much I loved
How much I cared.

You'll never know
About my pain,
About my broken heart.

You'll never know
How much I cried,
Just lying on my bed
And thinking...

You'll never know
How much I wish
How much I prayed
That things would go back

You'll never know
The emptiness that lies inside
That I wish would
Leave me...

Aphrodisiac

Arms pinned above my head
His hard body molded perfectly against my soft curves
Heavy breathing along my skin ,goose bumps appear across my flesh
His husky voice coated with lust speaking my name
My legs part with ease for him
His free hand traveling up the curve of my hip
My breath hitches in my throat
His hand continues up, the tips making my stomach clench
Traveling on his exploration of my body, his hand cups my breast
His thumb flicks over the harden bud
Heat fills my body, moisture pools south between my legs

He has me in the palm of his hand
My body is his for the taking
To do what he wants
My body and mind are lost to him

You know what

You know what?
I may be quiet and not talk to many people, that does not make me a
snob

You know what?
I am one of the most loyal people you would come across, but you
will never know it because you won't take the time to know me.

You know what?
I keep walls around me, protect myself, but that doesn't make me
weak

You know what?
Don't think you can take advantage of me just because I go out of my
way to help anyone that needs it

You know what?

Jennifer Dante

I'm tired of putting myself out there, breaking my walls to extend my hand in friendship to others only to get turned down

You know what?
Don't think you can come to me whenever you want or need something from me, that is not how a friendship works

You know what?
I may not be perfect, but neither are you, so take your lies and shove them up your "perfect" ass

You know what?
I'm done trying to make amends with certain friendships, if you really wanted to make it work, it would have been two-sided , not one-sided

Lastly, You know what?
Stay by myself because you know what kind of person a I am, and you accept me or leave me, I don't need wannabes in my life. I don't care!

Lost

What do you when all is lost
You can't find the rhythm or reason
to why it is happening to you
You are sicken to your stomach
by a punch you didn't see coming
You are looking to the past
for your answers to help you
and nothing is there
When moving one step forward
you feel rumbling chasing after you
taking a leap of faith
hoping something will catch you
Those that stood by you still stand by you
in the end when you need them the most

Pieces of a Broken Soul

that maybe not all is lost
They can see beyond the words
spoken falsely by others
And see you for who you truly are

With the help of those
I can stand up on my own
Pick up the pieces laid in the destruction
and move on.

If Only

If only...
I could disappear

If only...
I could not take things to heart

If only...
I was stronger

If only...
I could be a better person

If only...
I could learn from my mistakes

If only....
I could rely on myself and no other

If only...
I could change myself to please everyone

If only...
If only I could do all those things

Path

You ever feel lost in the world around you
Opening up doors only to come to a dead end
Changing paths thinking this could be the way
Only to come to a fork in the road

No matter North, South, East or West
They all lead to more roads with more directions
Or dead ends leaving you to turn around
That lost feeling never lessening or fading only to get strong

Soon you think it's better to give up then to keep going around in
circles

Will I?

Will I...
Will I ever fit in with others

Will I...
Feel like I can trust my friends

Will I...
Stop feeling let down and hurt by loved ones

Will I...
Feel like my friends are my true friends

Will I...
Ever rid myself of my demons

Will I...
Stop doubting the ones that supposedly care about me

Will I...
Be loved fully and completely by someone

Pieces of a Broken Soul

Will I...
Every find my place among everyone else

Will I...

Today

Today, at this every minute and second
You are where you are supposed to be
You are doing what is intended of you
Be happy

For tomorrow
It all changes
To something different
Something you don't want to do
Somewhere you don't want to be

The future is unknown for each one of us
So make the best of every situation
You are presented with
It might not be as bad as you think

Storm Warning

Be warned
A storm of emotions
Building up along the horizon
My screams are thunder
My anger is the lighting
My cries are the down pour of rain
My life is the wind, passing by

Jennifer Dante

Actions Speak

No need to speak
No need to explain

Your actions
Your motives

Show everything
Show the lies
Show the fake
Show the deceit

Missing the friendship
Missing the laughs
Missing what use to be

What was gained by your actions
Was worth what you have lost

A gorgeous chaos

She stands tall
Body lethal
With wicked curves
Wild dark hair whipping
Her creamy skin perfection
Wicked gleam in her eyes

A gorgeous chaos

Curl of her lip
A hand on her hip
Arch of her brow
Her voice low and raspy

A gorgeous chaos

Pieces of a Broken Soul

She stood looking to her peers
Those that wanted her to fail
She spoke her mind
Shocking all who heard

A gorgeous chaos

On the inside of herself
She's a mess
Walls breaking down around her
Once kept her safe
Vanish

A gorgeous chaos

In her eyes
She's fighting to keep from drowning
To stay calm
Her resolve cracking
Crumbling down around her

Look at her
She's a gorgeous chaos

Final Act

Rehearsals are behind us
Stage is ready, decorated in all its glamor
Final wardrobe check is complete
My knees are shaking
My palms sweating

This is the final curtain call
In this final episode
It's a solo act

This is my chance to make things right
Make things anew

Jennifer Dante

I see you in the crowd
Smiling back at me

I wanted a choice
This is not for me
I don't want to be alone
In the final scene

This is the final act
An encore will never happen
I hope you all enjoyed it
It was a good run while it lasted

I bow at the end
Fading into the darkness

More than I should

I care about you
More than I should
I treated you like gold
While I was treated like stone
Left out in the cold

After everything
My wish didn't come true
You will always remain a memory
Etched in my heart

Strong woman

A strong woman...
loves beyond all faults
wears her heart on her sleeve
picks of the pieces of someone that is broken
puts others first before herself

Pieces of a Broken Soul

A strong woman...
cries behind closed doors
falls apart when no one is looking
fights the battles no one else will
puts on a fake smile to show others she's fine

A strong woman...
can only be strong for so long
before everything comes crashing down around her
and only she knows how to pick up the pieces

Crux

Sweating out the sickness
Forcing all the demons and monsters down
I pick myself up off the floor
The pain slowly leaving me

I can still hear your words
taste them on my tongue
saying everything is fine
to make yourself feel better

It hurts to be alone
You were always supposed to me at my side
I don't know where it went wrong

I try to make sense of what's left of me
I can't keep myself together
I bite the bullet
Making a go of this alone

Jennifer Dante

Missing Pieces

Heartbroken
Completely lost
She would never be captured again

Time will pass soon
She will be strong enough
To break the chains that hold her down

Determined to rediscover herself
Her true nature
Find the missing pieces of her soul

She's not perfect

She's not perfect but She's worth it

She can be impatient
She can be insecure
She can make mistakes

She's not perfect but She's worth it

She will be a shoulder to cry on
She will be an ear to listen
She will be a shelter

She's not perfect but She's worth it

She can be forgetful
She can worry too much
She can forget to love herself

She's not perfect but She's worth it

She will make sure you are loved
She will make sure you are happy

Pieces of a Broken Soul

She will make sure you are appreciated

She's not perfect but She's worth it

She has her faults
She sees herself damaged
She will always wish could be more

She's not perfect but She's worth it

Brick

Brick by brick
The walls slowly come up

Around my heart
Around myself

Tried of hurting
Tried of trusting

Brick by brick
The walls slowly come up

Void of emotions
Void of love

Must protect my heart
Must protect myself

Brick by brick
The walls slowly come up

No one will ever enter them again

Jennifer Dante

Emotions

Hate
Anger
Rage

Jealous
Pain
Tears

Sadness
Regret
Bitter

Taking all these emotions
I place them inside a bottle

I no longer want them around me
Bringing me down more
When I should be lifting myself up.

Casting your name in the bottle
Along with all the emotions
I say my final good bye,
tossing it out into the ocean

I only want to keep the good memories
with me and in my heart

I need the room for new love and friendships

Happiness
Love
Laughter

Those are the emotions I need

Fool

I'm just a fool...
I believe your words

I'm just a fool..
I gave you everything

I'm just a fool...
I gave you my heart

I'm just a fool..
I thought you would always be there

I'm just a fool...
To think things could get better for us

I'm just a fool...
I didn't know you could be so cruel

I'm just a fool..
To think it was all my fault

Now I know better...
I won't let you hurt me again...

Only you

You came at the right time
When I felt like I had fallen from grace
You picked me, dusting me off

You have given me hope
When I was surround in darkness
I found the light in you

You gave me strength
When I was weak

Jennifer Dante

I could count on you for support

You gave me love
When I hated myself
You gave me a reason to live again

You gave me a map
When I was lost
I found my way back home

Hurricane

The day you walked into my life
You came in like hurricane
whisking me off my feet.
You caught my tears
wiping them off my cheeks
My heart slowly healed itself
You picked up the pieces
Putting it back together for me
I started to smile again
You were my reason
I felt whole again when I was with you
Now that I have you
I don't ever want to lose this feeling
There would be a special place
in my heart and soul for you
for as long as I live

Forever

Now and forever
Two souls
Bound together
Always in each other thoughts

No matter the distance
Always come back to each other
Drawn to each in our dreams and in our hearts

I melted your heart
You teased my senses
I loved you when you needed it
You became my joy

Now and forever
We are part of each other
No time nor space can change that

Forever Mine
Forever Yours

This time

This time
This moment

I'm not backing down
I'm not changing my mind
I'm standing up for myself
I'm doing things my way

Tried of the games
False dreams
Empty promises
Crying tears you don't deserve

Jennifer Dante

This time
This moment

I'm going back to myself
The girl I once was
The only girl I know

Second Chance

Fear now consumes me
My heart takes its last beat
My blood stops flowing
I can feel my soul screaming out
As it leaves my body

Don't leave me like this
Breath your life into me
Save me from death
I don't want to leave

Bring me back to life
Let your breath
Give me a second chance

Jealous

Green eyed monster
Like the devil himself
Creeps upon you
Slowing, digging its fingers
Preying on
weak of hearts
weak of minds
Jealousy starts its work
planting false ideas
playing on insecurities
Destroying
Plaguing
until nothing but ruins are left
the damage already done

It moves onto another victim

Steps

Three steps forward
Five steps back
Failure
Everything went south

Two steps forward
Six steps back
Frustration
Failed attempts

Four steps forward
Seven steps back
Disappointment
Things going the wrong way

One step forward
Seven steps back

Jennifer Dante

Misfortune
Feeling cursed

What's the point in trying
When you feel like it's
Not worth it anymore.

Enthralled

You
leave me breathless
from the intensity of our kiss
Your hunger to devour my body
heart, mind, and soul

Your
kiss renders me speechless
catching my breath afterwards
feasting on each other's body's
memorializing each touch
igniting the passion inside of me
I lose all sense of the moment

Walk over

Walk over my feet
So that I may never walk or run

Walk over my fingers
So that I may never touch or write again

Walk over my arms
So that I may never embrace or hug another

Walk over my lips
So that I may never speak again

Pieces of a Broken Soul

Walk over my eyes
So that I may never see again

Walk over my lungs
So that I may never breathe again

Walk over my heart
So that I may never love again

Walk all over me

Broken

Undress me
With your words
Tender touches
Remove the layers that shelter me
Gently and carefully
Layer after layer
Hurt and pain
Layer after layer
Scars and damage
Each layer removed
It burns and stings
Old wounds opening up once again
All the layers removed
Shattered heart
Fragile soul

Are you strong enough to help someone this broken?

Lover

Cherished in their arms
like a precious gift
Desire in their eyes
when looking at me
To feel their hunger
against my skin
Tasting their thirst
in our kisses
Bewitched by their words
spoken to me in my ear

I want this
from a lover

Demons

Demons slowly make their way just under the surface
They could feel her world slowly start to turn
Turn for the worse, this was their chance
Her armor once shielded her from everything negative
began to dull and tarnish, weakening its strong hold
The demons embedded their hooks
growing stronger while she grew weaker
Happiness replaced with grief
Love turned to bitterness
Demons thrived on vile emotions she felt
She once basked in lightness now hid from it
Darkness over took her
anger and hatred is what she knew
Demons reigned over her

No more

Deceitful words
Tarnished dreams

Holding onto for a change
You would be different this time
Second and third chances
given again and again

I deserve better
Given you everything
And in return I was given nothing

Death

Slipping away
slowly fading into oblivion
Death will be easy, painless
welcome it with open arms

Misery suffocates my heart
Grief strangles my soul
Trapped in the endless cycle of heartache

Gripping the blade tightly
First deep cut made
down the length of my arm
blood slowly seeps out

Mirror cut is made on the opposite side
Blood flows from my veins

The blade has done is job
Once warm body turns cold
Shadows dance across the walls
My heart pumps one last time

Jennifer Dante

Death calls me my name
My life is now his

Angel

I miss you
But I don't know even know you
You never met me
Death took you away before I was born
But I was born on your wedding anniversary
I have some of your belongings
You knew my name before I was born
I like to think you're my angel
Watching over me in this world

ABOUT THE AUTHOR

Jennifer was born and raised in Maryland. She is a single mother of a very active six year boy who is her heart. As a little girl, Jennifer always had a vivid imagination. It wasn't until high school that she found a love for art and everything to do with it. She won various awards for her art during her high school years. This path continued all the way through college where she earned her A.A. in web design.

Jennifer has been very lucky to visit historical art places over in Europe. Living near Washington D.C has also provided a chance to see various traveling art exhibits.

Her love of the arts has never stopped, and about three years ago she entered the world of writing. She met a few women that shared similar interest with her and have created stories together for their own amusement. With much encouragement from those women and friends, she decided venture out and show the world her writing.

Reach Jennifer Here

https://www.facebook.com/JenniferDanteAuthor
https://www.facebook.com/jennifer.dante.980
http://jenniferdante.blogspot.com
jennifer.dante82@gmail.com

www.ingramcontent.com/pod-product-compliance
Lightning Source LLC
Chambersburg PA
CBHW071751020426
42331CB00008B/2280